Set.setsíntns re Stsmémelt

(Children's Songs)

Translations by Mona Jules

Translations
Mona Jules
Secwepemc Cultural Education Society

Illustrations
Dave Seymour
Kamloops Band

Colour
Lizzy Ignace
Skeetchestn Indian Band / Secwepemc Nation

Editor
Sarah Kell
First Peoples' Cultural Foundation

2005

Order this book online at www.trafford.com
or email orders@trafford.com

Most Trafford titles are also available at major online book retailers.

Trafford
PUBLISHING®   www.trafford.com
North America & international
toll-free: 844 688 6899 (USA & Canada)
fax: 812 355 4082

Our mission is to efficiently provide the world's finest, most comprehensive book publishing service, enabling every author to experience success. To find out how to publish your book, your way, and have it available worldwide, visit us online at www.trafford.com

Because of the dynamic nature of the Internet, any web addresses or links contained in this book may have changed since publication and may no longer be valid. The views expressed in this work are solely those of the author and do not necessarily reflect the views of the publisher, and the publisher hereby disclaims any responsibility for them.

Any people depicted in stock imagery provided by Getty Images are models, and such images are being used for illustrative purposes only.
Certain stock imagery © Getty Images.

ISBN: 978-1-4120-6569-6 (sc)
ISBN: 978-1-6987-1065-5 (e)

Print information available on the last page.

Trafford rev. 12/16/2021

Table of Contents

Weyt-k

Hello

Weyt-k.	Hello.
Lé7en-k ̓tucw?	Are you in good health?
Weyt-k.	Hello.
Lé7en-k ̓tucw?	Are you in good health?
Weyt-k.	Hello.
Lé7en-k ̓tucw?	Are you in good health?
Pyin te sitq̓t.	Today?
Mé7e lél7e-ken.	Yes, I'm in good health.
Mé7e lél7e-ken.	Yes, I'm in good health.
Mé7e lél7e-ken.	Yes, I'm in good health.
Pyin te sitq̓t.	Today.

Xwexwistsín

Valentine Song

(Sing to a tune from any favourite song children like.)
(Children hold up their fingers to represent their family.)

Xwexwistéten re pepé7 ell   I like father and
Xwexwistéten re méme7.   I like mother.

Xwexwistéten re kic ell   I like big sister and
Xwexwistéten re qetsk.   I like big brother.

Xwexwistéten re síntse ell   I like little brother and
Xwexwistéten re tsétse.   I like little sister.

Xwexwistéten re skúye ell   I like baby and
Xwexwistéten re méme7.   I like mother.

Xwexwistéten re kyé7e ell   I like grandmother and
Xwexwistéten re xpé7e.   I like grandfather.

Nehé7e lu7 re Sḱépqen?

Where is the Head?

(Tune: In and Out the Window)

Nehé7e lu7 re sḱépqen?

Nehé7e lu7 re sḱépqen?

Nehé7e lu7 re sḱépqen?

Nehé7e lu7 re sḱépqen?

Where is the head?

(Children point to the head.)

Nehé7e lu7 re qéwten?

Nehé7e lu7 re qéwten?

Nehé7e lu7 re qéwten?

Nehé7e lu7 re qéwten?

Where is the hair?

(Children point to the hair.)

Nehé7e lu7 re ckwt̓ústen?

Nehé7e lu7 re ckwt̓ústen?

Nehé7e lu7 re ckwt̓ústen?

Nehé7e lu7 re ckwt̓ústen?

Where are the eyes?

(Children point to the eyes.)

Nehé7e lu7 re sṗseqs?

Nehé7e lu7 re sṗseqs?

Nehé7e lu7 re sṗseqs?

Nehé7e lu7 re sṗseqs?

Where is the nose?

(Children point to the nose.)

(Repeat this pattern, incorporating the rest of the body parts.)

ʼténe	ear
splútsen	mouth
kwellkʼmúse7	cheek
sqʼwext	legs
pʼúsmen	heart
xwqwyépstn	neck
kelc	hand
skwʼtus	face
tkʼmíscen̓	forehead
tkʼemtsín̓	lips
tkʼmépe7sqen	chin
tícwe7tsk	tongue
tsepllóy̓e	eyelashes
tkʼétmúy̓e	eyebrows
qu7	navel

O Skwenkwínem

Nature Song

O skwenkwínem   O skwenkwínem   (wild potatoes)
O ho ho ho ho ho   O ho ho ho ho ho

O re pétse   O re pétse   (digging stick)
O ho ho ho ho ho   O ho ho ho ho ho

O re miṁc   O re miṁc   (birch bark basket)
O ho ho ho ho ho   O ho ho ho ho ho

O re scwicw   O re scwicw   (avalanche lily)
O ho ho ho ho ho   O ho ho ho ho ho

O re sxúsem   O re sxúsem   (soapberries)
O ho ho ho ho ho   O ho ho ho ho ho

O speqpeq7úẃi   O speqpeq7úẃi   (saskatoons)
O ho ho ho ho ho   O ho ho ho ho ho

O re spélem   O re spélem   (meadow)
O ho ho ho ho ho   O ho ho ho ho ho

O re pésellkwe   O re pésellkwe   (lake)
O ho ho ho ho ho   O ho ho ho ho ho

O re setétkwe   O re setétkwe   (river)
O ho ho ho ho ho   O ho ho ho ho ho

Thé7en lu7 le Fern?

Where is Fern?
(Tune: Frère Jacques)

Children form a circle and dance. As each child's name is called, he or she enters the circle. Repeat the song with each child's name.

Thé7en lu7 le Fern?	Where is Fern?
Thé7en lu7 le Fern?	Where is Fern?
Ye7éne le Fern.	Here is Fern. (Teacher points to Fern.)
Ye7éne le Fern.	Here is Fern.
Tsxwénte pyin me7 séyse-kt.	Come everyone, let's play.
Tsxwénte pyin me7 séyse-kt.	Come everyone, let's play.
Weyt-k Fern.	Hello Fern.
Weyt-k Fern.	Hello Fern.
La la la. La la la.	

9

Stémi k Llcwentéc?

What Did You Wear?

Stémi k llcwentéc?	What did you wear?
Stémi k llcwentéc?	What did you wear?
Stémi k llcwentéc?	What did you wear?
Pyin te sitqt.	Today?
Swéti7 k pell-stektíts'e7?	Who has a shirt?
Swéti7 k pell-stektíts'e7? Ts'elíl-ce.	(Those wearing shirts stand up.)
Stémi k llcwentéc?	What did you wear?
Stémi k llcwentéc?	What did you wear?
Stémi k llcwentéc?	What did you wear?
Pyin te sitqt.	Today?
Swéti7 k pell-sxétemcen?	Who has on jeans?
Swéti7 k pell-sxétemcen? Ts'elíl-ce.	(Those wearing jeans stand up.)

Swéti7 k pell-ckúpcen̓?	Who has socks on?
Swéti7 k pell-ckúpcen̓? Ts'elíl-ce.	(Those wearing socks stand up.)

Stém̓i k llcwentéc?	What did you wear?
Stém̓i k llcwentéc?	What did you wear?
Stém̓i k llcwentéc?	What did you wear?
Pyin te sitq̓t.	Today?

Swéti7 k pell-síllts'u?	Who has shoes on?
Swéti7 k pell-síllts'u? Ts'elíl-ce.	(Those wearing shoes stand up.)

(Continue learning other articles of clothing and adornments.)

qmut	hat
mémle	necklace
tkweltkél̓eqs	underwear
kikyéne	earring
cqléẃten	purse
llellúcw / lekepú	coat
spéke7	gloves
píl̓ce	skirt
cllucwpéxen	vest

W7ec Nck̓méles re Skéki7.

There's a Spider on the Floor.

The Language Teacher brings in a spider and demonstrates each part of the body mentioned as the students sing the song.

Neréy re skéki7 w7ec nxlílep, nxlílep.   There's a spider on the floor.

Neréy re skéki7 w7ec nxlílep, nxlílep.

Pyin re skéki7 w7ec nsq̓wext, nsq̓wext.   Now it's on the foot.

Pyin re skéki7 w7ec nsq̓wext, nsq̓wext.

Pyin re skéki7 w7ec nwelánk, nwelánk.   Now it's on the tummy.

Pyin re skéki7 w7ec nwelánk, nwelánk.

Pyin re skéki7 w7ec nxwqwyépstn, nxwqwyépstn.   Now it's on the neck.

Pyin re skéki7 w7ec nxwqwyépstn, nxwqwyépstn.

Pyin re skéki7 w7ec nskw̓tus, nskw̓tus.   This time the spider is on the face.

Pyin re skéki7 w7ec nskw̓tus, nskw̓tus.

Pyin re skéki7 w7ec nqéwten, nqéwten.   This time the spider is on the hair.

Pyin re skéki7 w7ec nqéwten, nqéwten.

Re m-llwilc nxlílep re skéki7.   The spider jumped to the floor.

Re m-llwilc nxlílep re skéki7.

Sk̓épqen, T̓kméne

Head and Shoulders

Children touch each part of the body mentioned as they sing along.

Sk̓épqen ell t̓kméne,	Head and shoulders,
Sk̓méẃistcen ell lexlíxcen,	Knees and toes,
Sk̓méẃistcen ell lexlíxcen.	Knees and toes.
Sk̓épqen ell t̓kméne,	Head and shoulders,
Sk̓méẃistcen ell lexlíxcen,	Knees and toes,
Sk̓méẃistcen ell lexlíxcen.	Knees and toes.

13

Élkwentiye

Put Away
(Tune: Mary had a Little Lamb)

The Language Teacher praises the ones who are doing a good job, to encourage others.

Élkwentiye re sisyékstn, sisyékstn, sisyékstn.	Put away the toys.
Élkwentiye re sisyékstn, stétme7cwiye.	Hurry up.
Yerí7 e sxexé7 Rodney, Rodney, Rodney.	You are a great helper,
Yerí7 e sxexé7 Rodney.	Rodney.
Élkwentiye re sisyékstn, sisyékstn, sisyékstn.	Put away the toys.
Élkwentiye re sisyékstn, stétme7cwiye.	Hurry up.

14

Re Sqélemcw te W7ec Ncḱmém̓les

Farmer in the Dell

Form a circle with joined hands, one boy in the centre to be the farmer. He takes a wife, the wife takes a child, the child takes a big sister, the big sister takes a dog.

Re sqélemcw mut ntsitcws,	The man lives in his house,
Re sqélemcw mut ntsitcws,	The man lives in his house,
La la la la la la,	La la la la la la,
Re sqélemcw mut ntsitcws.	The man lives in his house.
Re sqélemcw kwnem te sem7é7em,	The man takes a wife.
Re sqélemcw kwnem te sem7é7em,	
La la la la la la,	
Re sqélemcw kwnem te sem7é7em.	
Re sem7é7em kwnem te skúye,	The wife takes a child.
Re sem7é7em kwnem te skúye,	
La la la la la la,	
Re sem7é7em kwnem te skúye.	
Re skúye kwnem te kic,	The child takes a big sister.
Re skúye kwnem te kic,	
La la la la la la,	
Re skúye kwnem te kic.	
Re kic kwnem te sqéxe,	Big sister takes a dog.
Re kic kwnem te sqéxe,	
La la la la la la,	
Re kic kwnem te sqéxe.	

Swúcwtmucw

Snowman

Children form a circle with joined hands. One child in the centre is the snowman.
Children dance around the snowman and chant: One falls down! The snowman counts
the remaining children, then one falls down again. The counting begins again until there
are no more children to be counted. Begin again with another snowman in the centre,
counting from 10 to 1.

Re swúcwtmucw sts'lewt ne swucwt.

Úpekst te stsmémelt ec siséysus.

Tnk̓we7 estkíc ne swucwt ... cu! ... cu!

Pyin tkwínk̓wenc tek stsmémelt

K w7ec k siséysus ne swucwt?

Snowman standing in the snow.

Ten children playing.

One fell down!

Now how many are there

Playing in the snow?

Re swúcwtmucw sts'lewt ne swucwt.

Temllenkúk̓w7e te stsmémelt ec siséysus.

Tnk̓we7 estkíc ne swucwt ... cu! ... cu!

Pyin tkwínk̓wenc tek stsmémelt

K w7ec k siséysus ne swucwt?

Snowman standing in the snow.

Nine children playing.

One fell down!

Now how many are there

Playing in the snow?

Re swúcwtmucw sts'lewt ne swucwt.

Tnek̓w7ú7ps te stsmémelt ec siséysus.

Tnk̓we7 estkíc ne swucwt ... cu! ... cu!

Pyin tkwínk̓wenc tek stsmémelt

K w7ec k siséysus ne swucwt?

Snowman standing in the snow.

Eight children playing.

One fell down!

Now how many are there

Playing in the snow?

Stémi ke7 Swíkem?

What Do You See?

The Language Teacher holds up objects or pictures of animals, birds and other themes and asks, for example, "Cat, cat, what do you see?" Children respond with the answers.

Pus, pus stémi ke7 swíkem?   Cat, cat, what do you see?
Wíkem te spyu7.   He sees a bird.

Sqéxe, sqéxe stémi ke7 swíkem?   Dog, dog, what do you see?
Wíkem te pus.   He sees a cat.

Nts'e7sqéxe7, nts'e7sqéxe7   Horse, horse, what do you see?
   stémi ke7 swíkem?
Wíkem te sqéxe.   He sees a dog.

Vocabulary

sníne	owl
squwéy	blue-jay
k̓wsicw	goose
cméye	house fly
sqlu7úẃi	beaver
estsék̓	squirrel
teníye	moose
ts'i7	deer

W7ec re Xílmes

This is How They Go.

Children walk around and sing: "This is what the rabbit does." As they sing, they hop, indicating how the rabbit hops. Incorporate other animals.

W7ec re xílmes t̓7éne re sqwyits	This is what the rabbit does,
Re sqwyits, re sqwyits,	The rabbit, the rabbit.
Llegw, llegw, llegw.	Hop, hop, hop.
W7ec re xílmes t̓7éne re spipyúy̓e	This is what the birds do,
Re spipyúy̓e, re spipyúy̓e,	The birds, the birds.
Ts'ligw, ts'ligw, ts'ligw.	Scratch, scratch, scratch.
W7ec re xílmes t̓7éne re squwéy	This is what the blue-jays do,
Re squwéy, re squwéy,	The blue-jays, the blue-jays.
T̓ucwt, t̓ucwt, t̓ucwt.	Fly, fly, fly.
W7ec re xelxílmes-kucw,	This is what we do.
Séyse, séyse, séyse.	Play, play, play.

K̓woyí7ese te Skék̓i7

Itsy Bitsy Spider

Children hold out their thumbs and forefingers, touching the thumb of one hand and changing over to the other thumb to represent the spider climbing. They raise their arms and wiggle their fingers as they lower their arms to their sides, representing the spider floating away. They raise their arms, forming a circle above their heads to represent the sun. Repeat the actions.

K̓woyí7ese te skék̓i7
m-répelc lu7 ntsrep.

Little spider
climbs up a tree.

Tser7épes re skllékstem,
m-kwéwtes re skék̓i7.

Rain storm washes
spider away.

Re m-tskwték̓es re skwék̓w7es
m-xwúlecwes re tmicw.

When the sun comes up,
the earth dries up.

K̓woyí7ese te skék̓i7
m-répelc cú7tsem.

Little spider
climbs up a tree once more.

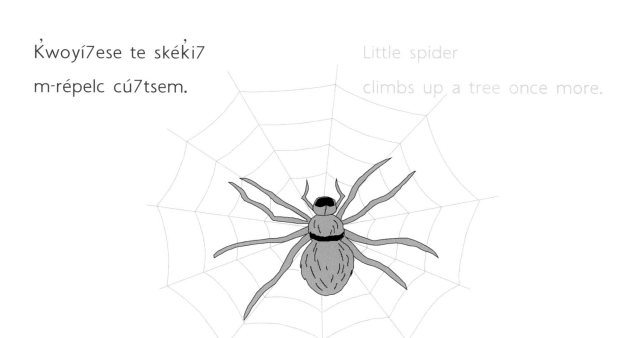

Tsítselkst te Sqexqexe7éẏe

Five Little Puppies

Children chant and act out the story.

Tsítselkst te sqexqexe7éẏe ec re llegwllegwiĺcwes nspúĺten.
Nekúḱw7e m-ḱwellciyúcwt m-xen7épqnes.
Re kí7ce tsqwlentés re Docta.
Re Docta m-tsut:
Ta7 k sqexqexe7éẏe me7 llegwllegwiĺcs ne k spúĺten.

Mums te sqexqexe7éẏe ec re llegwllegwiĺcwes nspúĺten.
Nekúḱw7e m-ḱwellciyúcwt m-xen7épqnes.
Re kí7ce tsqwlentés re Docta.
Re Docta m-tsut:
Ta7 k sqexqexe7éẏe me7 llegwllegwiĺcs ne k spúĺten.

Kellélls te sqexqexe7éẏe ec re llegwllegwiĺcwes nspúĺten.
Nekúḱw7e m-ḱwellciyúcwt m-xen7épqnes.
Re kí7ce tsqwlentés re Docta.
Re Docta m-tsut:
Ta7 k sqexqexe7éẏe me7 llegwllegwiĺcs ne k spúĺten.

Sesésle te sqexqexe7éẏe ec re llegwllegwiĺcwes nspúĺten.
Nekúḱw7e m-ḱwellciyúcwt m-xen7épqnes.
Re kí7ce tsqwlentés re Docta.
Re Docta m-tsut:
Ta7 k sqexqexe7éẏe me7 llegwllegwiĺcs ne k spúĺten.

Nekúk̓w7e te sqexe7éy̓e ec re llegwllegwil̓cwes nspúl̓ten.

Re m̓-k̓wellciyúcwt m̓-xen7épqnes.

Re kí7ce tsqwlentés re Docta.

Re Docta m̓-tsut:

Ta7 k sqexqexe7éy̓e me7 llegwllegwíl̓cs ne k spúl̓ten.

English Version

Five little puppies jumping on the bed.
One fell from the bed and hurt his head.
Mother called the Doctor in.
The Doctor said:
No little puppies are to jump on the bed.

(Continue counting in reverse order to number one.)

21

Nsqepts

In the Spring

Children raise their hands and wiggle their fingers to indicate leaves growing. They raise their hands slowly to represent the grass growing. They cup their hands to indicate the flowers growing, and they pretend to build a nest.

K̓ult re ptsekll, k̓ult re ptsekll.	Leaves are sprouting ...
Nsqepts, nsqepts.	In the spring, in the spring.
K̓ult re ptsekll.	Leaves are sprouting.
K̓ult re kwlékwle, k̓ult re kwlékwle.	Grass is growing ...
Nsqepts, nsqepts.	In the spring, in the spring.
K̓ult re kwlékwle.	Grass is growing.
K̓ult re segwlén̓sem,	Flowers are blooming ...
k̓ult re segwlén̓sem.	
Nsqepts, nsqepts.	In the spring, in the spring.
K̓ult re segwlén̓sem.	Flowers are blooming.
K̓úlem te c7ú7setn re spiyúy̓e,	Birds are building nests ...
re spiyúy̓e.	
Nsqepts, nsqepts.	In the spring, in the spring.
K̓úlem te c7ú7setn.	Birds are building nests.
Re weswísxen tcúsem te s7íllen.	Robins are looking for food.
Nsqepts, nsqepts.	In the spring, in the spring.

Re kenkéknem qillt ell tsektsíkme7kst. Bears wake up and stretch.
Nsqepts, nsqepts. In the spring, in the spring.

M7ixw re scúyent. The ice melts.
Nsqepts, nsqepts. In the spring, in the spring.

Gwesgwást, gwesgwást, Sunshine, sunshine,
Gwesgwást, gwesgwást. Sunshine, sunshine.

Re skéki7 íllens re cméye. The spider eats a fly.
Nsqepts. In the spring.

Swúcwtmucw

Snowman

Children stand and pretend to be the snowman. They put their hands up to represent tall hats and they point to their eyes, nose, mouth and neck as they chant. They form a circle with their arms over their heads to represent the sun. Children slowly collapse to represent the melting snowman.

Swucwtmúmc-ken.	I'm a snowman.
Tsqmúmt-ken te xyum.	I'm wearing a big hat.
Sqelqelélx ncwkwetkwtútstn.	My eyes are made of buttons.
Geyú7 nspsesqs.	My nose is a carrot.
Pell cts'qú7etn nsplúltsen.	There's a pipe in my mouth.
Tsiqw nxwqwetiyépstn.	My scarf is red.
Tskwtek re skwékw7es.	The sun rises.
Ená te7!	Oh no!
Me7 m7í7xw-ken.	I'm going to melt.

24

Printed in the United States
by Baker & Taylor Publisher Services